Business As Usual

*A step-by-step guide for female entrepreneurs **to building their online business***

Nadine Bryant

© Copyright May 2020 by <u>Nadine Bryant</u> - All rights reserved.

This document is geared towards providing exact and reliable information in regards to the topic and issue covered. The publication is sold with the idea that the publisher is not required to render accounting, officially permitted, or otherwise, qualified services. If advice is necessary, legal or professional, a practiced individual in the profession should be ordered.

- From a Declaration of Principles which was accepted and approved equally by a Committee of the American Bar Association and a Committee of Publishers and Associations.

In no way is it legal to reproduce, duplicate, or transmit any part of this document in either electronic means or in printed format. Recording of this publication is strictly prohibited and any storage of this document is not allowed unless with written permission from the publisher. All rights reserved.

The information provided herein is stated to be truthful and consistent, in that any liability, in terms of inattention or otherwise, by any usage or abuse of any policies, processes, or directions contained within is the solitary and utter responsibility of the recipient reader. Under no circumstances will any legal responsibility or blame be held against the publisher for any reparation, damages, or monetary loss due to the information herein, either directly or indirectly.

Respective authors own all copyrights not held by the publisher.

The information herein is offered for informational purposes solely, and is universal as so. The presentation of the information is without contract or any type of guarantee assurance.

The trademarks that are used are without any consent, and the publication of the trademark is without permission or backing by the trademark owner. All trademarks and brands within this book are for clarifying purposes only and are the owned by the owners themselves, not affiliated with this document.

Table of Contents

Introduction	9
Chapter 1 – Getting started	13
Chapter 2 – What's your niche?	19
Chapter 3 – Branding	23
Chapter 4 – Registering your business	30
Chapter 5 – Let's talk Capital Investment	38
Chapter 6 – Accounting and Banking	42
Chapter 7 – Marketing	46
Chapter 8 – Staying the course	52
Conclusion	56

INTRODUCTION

I wanted to express my sincere thanks and congratulations on taking the first step to become a successful female entrepreneur.

My intention with this book is to encourage aspiring female entrepreneurs (of any age) to take the first steps in building and launching their online business.

This book will guide you through a step-by-step process from your first idea all the way through to building your own empire.

Money does not grow on trees, but since the turn of the millennium, it has been sprouting on the Internet. Today, the Internet has made more millionaires than any other field. Opportunities abound for anyone sufficiently motivated to carve a niche for herself and earn on the Internet.

The increase in online opportunities has also coincided with an increase in the number of female-owned businesses. Gone are the old times when women were cast in a stereotype that made it hard for them to aspire for business success. To a large extent, gone are the old customs that made women seem incapable of setting up their brand. Today, women have proven that they can compete favourably with men when the grounds are level. In 2017 alone, for instance, women were responsible for creating 9million jobs and contributed $1.7 trillion in revenue to the U.S economy. In fact, women start new businesses at 1.5 times the usual rate in the developed world.

Sadly though, the odds say most businesses are likely to fail than succeed, and that includes online businesses run by women.

Many research studies have shown that 90% of online businesses fail within the first one hundred and twenty days, and when you add to that the problems that female entrepreneurs face, you may be forgiven for being sceptical about your chances out there on the world wide web.

Are you looking for a worthwhile endeavour to turn your inner strength towards? Do you have a cause you want to promote? Are you worried you may be competing against a stacked field? Are you concerned that established competitors may squeeze out your start-up?

Well, these are all valid concerns, and they are why I have written this book for you – to show you the principles you must hold dear as you strike out in the online business world as a woman.

Why do I think every woman has it in them to eke out a living in online business?

Many women have distinguished themselves and gone on to create awesome business entities that have lasted the test of time.

What did they know that most female entrepreneurs don't know? What mindset enabled them to defeat the odds and record repeated success? What are the most common mistakes female entrepreneurs make that reduce their chances of success?

The answers to these questions form the main thrust of this book. To become successful, you need (1) the right mindset, and (2) the right knowledge. Most entrepreneurs lack one or the other. That is the main reason most businesses crash.

In this book, I will arm you with the basic essentials you must know as a female business-builder, and teach you the right kind of mindset that will allow your brand to flourish beyond even your expectations.

I only ask for one thing – that you read every line and tip with the desire to incorporate it into your daily schedule as you look to create a success story. In return, I promise to give you enough actionable knowledge to build first your mindset, and then your business.

Once again, thank you from the bottom of my heart for reading this book. I hope it brings you great success and sets you on the path to turning your passion into your empire.

CHAPTER 1
Getting Started

Charting a new path for female entrepreneurs

In the twenty years between 1997 and 2017, the number of women-controlled business increased by 114 percent, at a rate bigger than the worldwide rate. That meant that more females were willing to throw their hats in the ring and compete even in industries traditionally dominated by men.

However, female entrepreneurship did not just start at the beginning of this millennium. A far back as the 18th century, Eliza Lucas Pinckney took over her family plantation and recorded successes running the establishment, a role usually reserved for males. Many cultures, including the traditional Australian society, frowned upon women running businesses, but still, notable names like Rebecca Lukens flourished despite the prejudice.

At the beginning of the twentieth century, Madam C. J. Walker became the first recognised female millionaire, and female entrepreneurship has not looked back since then across the world. Today, names like Oprah Winfrey, Diane Hendricks, Meg Whitman, Anna Wright, Olivia Molesworth, and Katie Page bear the flag, but admittance is open for anyone committed and motivated enough to join the ranks of successful female entrepreneurs. The greatest lure for you as a female entrepreneur, like other entrepreneurs, is the chance to be your own boss, defining terms and rules of business engagements. Few things come close to the satisfaction of knowing you are able to chart new territories and build the capacity to pursue every worthwhile idea you get.

However, even though the Mastercard Index of Women Entrepreneurs ranks Australia eighth in the world for the total percentage of women-owned businesses worldwide, there are still several potential threats you may need to overcome to leave your mark.

- **Social expectations**

The world has certainly done better in equalising the stakes, but the business world is still very much dominated by men. Certain stereotypes still exist, and it's going to take some time to tear them all down. For instance, the typical image people conjure when they hear the term "CEO" is most commonly male. It's no longer a novel idea, but most people still have to take a few moments readjusting their expectations when introduced to a female business owner.

If that does not jar you, consider the fact that a higher percentage of men dominate almost all business symposiums. It's not something to stop any serious entrepreneur, but social expectations can give you a few unpleasant surprises along the way.

- **Reduced access to funding**

A 2014 **report** stated that less than 3% of companies that were funded by venture capital had females as their CEO. This agrees with other reports that had cited 7%. Whatever the case, it is clear that more male-led companies receive funding access. Perhaps, this is best explained by the fact that men seem to dominate venture capital panels.

- **Difficulty building a support network**

Almost half of all female entrepreneurs have **said** that they had difficulties establishing a support network to support their ideas. In the business world, like poles attract when it comes to mentorship, and that explains why it is harder for women to source for mentors, advisors, and build a support network.

- **Combining business and family life**

In more ways than less, women are still saddled with the greater responsibility of directing the affairs at homes. Combining these responsibilities with an active business life may prove too difficult or hard without the right support systems in place. This is yet another obstacle you may need to deal with.

Why Online Businesses?
I mean, we have agreed that female entrepreneurs are killing it, but why do you specifically need an online business?
Well, I invite you to look at the following brands and tell me the common thing among them besides the fact that they are leading brands in their online niche – Huffington post, TPG, Flickr, Lifehacker, Blogger, Blurb, and Net-A-Porter.
Did you provide the right answer? Yes!
They were all founded or led by women. That means there is a space for women in the online world. That means there is space for you at the top of the online business world, and the lines between genders are better blurred.
Here are a few more specific reasons why you should consider an online business.

- **Low start-up costs.** Depending on the business idea and technical expertise you have, an online business may require next to zero capital. Most online giants, even Facebook and Twitter, started as pet projects that required little capital. Of course, as you expand and grow, you may need to source for more capital, but at least, starting the business is not cost-intensive.

- **Less overhead costs.** There is no requirement for extra staff or physical workspace, and that will help you save a lot on overhead costs. Even when you choose to outsource part of your work, you are going to pay fewer dollars to get it done compared to the running expenses you would have incurred setting up an offline business.

- **Flexibility.** Women are particularly drawn towards online businesses due to the flexibility they offer. With nobody breathing down your neck, you can switch working hours, pick extra jobs, or create more time for your family. You can also choose where and when you want to work. You practically become your own boss from the first day.

- **Easy exposure.** For an offline brand based in Melbourne to expand its reach to Sydney, a lot may have to go into promotion and branding, in terms of costs and efforts. The Internet can take you on that same journey at a cheaper and less labour-intensive rate.

- **A wide choice of business ideas.** The Internet is constantly rewarding people that can answer old questions in new ways or provide smarter solutions. *Uber* is a great example. We were used to taxi cabs, but when *Uber* introduced e-hailing, they disrupted an existing system and got rewarded for it. There is no end in sight to questions you can provide smarter solutions for, to eke out a space for your brand.

It is not all plain sailing for online businesses, though. They also have certain general drawbacks that you should take into account. Nothing you cannot fix, but you should definitely take one more look at them.

- **Fraud.** Sadly, not everyone on the other side of the screen has honest intentions. Security is left in the hands of every internet user to a large extent, and you have to stay vigilant to ensure you do not lose money or even your work, to fraud.

- **Technical issues and support.** Digital literacy rates differ among individuals. Well, we all run into one bug we cannot deal with on our own. Or you may need new software for your brand. The point I am making is that sooner rather than later, you are going to need technical assistance to asset up and manage an online business. While most issues are going to be minor fixes that a Google search will take care of, others may need more hands-on touches from a professional. That increases your expenses and your turn-around-time.

- **More competition.** This is a no-brainer, really. You are not the only one thinking of an online business. In fact, many businesses are started on the net daily. I have already mentioned that most die a natural, quick death, but while they exist, they add to the field you have to compete against. Throw in the big, established brands, and you realise just how big a task is ahead of you.

The Most Important Factor

What is the most important determinant of success and failure that you need to take care of? You! Or, more accurately, your mindset.

The human mind is the most fertile piece of real estate on Planet Earth. It takes whatever thoughts we put in it, and multiplies it. So, if you possess a scarcity mindset, you will find it incredibly hard to get started. You will always find excuses and theories for why your ideas cannot work. You will shoot down your *perfect* plans before you have even taken the first step.

As basic requirements, you must have healthy levels of, (1) Confidence (2) Perseverance and (3) Positivity

Confidence comes with self-esteem and competence. Self-esteem teaches you to expect good things to happen to you. You need to feel worthy of the success you want or it will continue to elude you. Being female matters less and less daily, and that's enough excuse for you not to succeed.

You also need some level of competence. You are not going to win an Olympic Gold next year if you cannot swim at a professional level now, and you do not plan to start training anytime soon.

Combined together, self-esteem and competence will give you the required confidence to take on problems and solve them.

You also need to persevere. The road to success is filled with bumps and pits. You cannot stop at each bump or turn back at every pit. No, you must learn to forge ahead despite obstacles in your path. Setbacks and failures will occur, but you need to prime yourself for a fresh assault.

You also need a lot of positivity. A positive mindset emphasises solutions rather than excuses, optimism rather than pessimism. The business world is already hard without you shooting yourself in the foot. When you host a destructive voice in your head, belittling every step you take, it's going to be hard to make any progress. So, make some space for positivity.

CHAPTER 2
What's your niche?

What you choose to do online is very important to the success of your business too. There are a wide variety of online businesses, and you need to decide what you want to model your business around. Here is where most people get it wrong. They either choose something they like doing without finding out if it will sell. Or they choose a hot niche they have no passion for. That is also wrong.

There are so many niches and ideas out there that you will surely find something that interests you and has a market value if you show enough patience.

Passion for your niche is non-negotiable – and you need to brainstorm to find something that fits your vision and interest.

Here are some common businesses that thrive online. You can see if you have an interest in any.

- **Car/Home Rental Service.** Running a rental service is a niche that thrives particularly well in a densely-populated area. It is even better if you have a large flow of people either because you are close to a major airport/terminal or a steady flow of tourists. As you might have noticed, this may not be totally online, but the bookings and reservations aspect can definitely be taken online. Here is where it gets even more interesting. You do not even need to own any of the cars or homes. You can simply serve as the bridge between owners and potential users. You win either way.

- **Self-publishing.** Self-publishing is the new domain flipping. In the early 2000s, domain flipping was the in-thing. You could buy domain names cheaply and then flip them over for huge profits. Today, self-publishing a book with online platforms like Amazon KDP is so easy. You do not even have to write the books yourself – you can hire freelance artists for that. Ads are not compulsory, but they will help you gain even better traction. When properly approached, self-publishing is an enriching business venture that anyone can start.

- **Ads Management.** Okay, this requires some initial technical knowledge. You need to learn how search engines work and how to tweak the algorithm to your needs. Why? Many people have products to sell and are willing to pay the right person that can help them set up marketing campaigns that reach the targeted audience. Understanding concepts such as SEM, SEO, and PPC will help you set up an agency that can help clients rank higher in search indexes and bring their products closer to the consumers.

- **Software development.** If you do not have the capital to start, this may be a bit hard unless you have learnt programming languages that you can leverage to create software solutions for your clients. Daily, businesses require new software and packages to deliver their service. You can set up a business to cater to their diverse needs. There is certainly a market for that.

- **Web Design.** This is closely aligned to the last point. Website design will never run out of fashion for as long as the Internet exists. A website design business can be tailored to help clients connect better with their consumer base and prospective leads.

- **Blogging.** This is perhaps the most common route

people choose. However, not everyone makes it to the very top simply because there are so many blogs around. You must be willing to stand out by the quality of content you deliver, the niche you have chosen, and monetisation routes.

This is only a sneak peek of business ideas you can choose to try out. There are still many more out there.

However, as I have said, your passion should guide you to choose the right business. You also need to look around you.

What are the questions that people need answered? What are the novel solutions you can provide? How can you simplify existing protocols? How can you bring smarter steps to everyday activities?

When you find the answers to this, make them your Unique Selling Points – the thing you do that other people don't do. Your USPs will help you stay ahead of the competition, and become an integral part of your brand.

You also need to know what sort of product or service you want to offer.

Are you going to run a reservations agency?

Are you going to open an online retail store?

Do you want to create courses and sell them online?

Answer these questions, and you would be on the way already.

Market research

Next up is market research. You cannot just think of a business idea, and then launch it. No! That's a shortcut to nowhere. You need to understand the market and who you are competing with. How many businesses already offer rental services? Is the market large enough for your offering? What is your plan for taking over a share of the market that has belonged to another business?

Market research will bring you up to date on current trends and entry points for your strategy. You can then plan from there.

Set Your Goals

As Bill Copeland put it, "The trouble with not having a goal is that you can spend your life running up and down the field and never score." So, you need a vision to guide you towards success. You will be surprised at how many people do not even bother to set goals.

What is your vision? What is the one thing you desire above all? What would make you completely satisfied? Creating a logistics company that will handle half of the haulage in your city? It's certainly achievable with the right commitment. But then, a long-term vision is not enough. It is too far away to command immediate motivation and commitment. To counter this, you need to break your long-term goals into short-term goals and milestones. Our mind often procrastinates, and if you choose big, complex goals, you may find yourself using that as an excuse for inaction.

If your goal is to go into self-publishing, do not just start with visions of earning a six-figure monthly income. Instead, break that goal down into smaller milestones and watch it becomes easier to break successive milestones rather than focus on one big, overwhelming vision.

Developing a business plan

A business plan is a document that highlights the route you plan to take to your goals. Consider it a map to follow towards your final target. A good business plan contains the details about your business idea and the requirements for achieving your business goals.

Why do you need a business plan?

A business plan can serve as a measure of your progress towards your goal. It can be the GPS that shows you how much still needs to be done to get to your target. Developing a business plan will also help you identify most of the weaknesses of your idea and potential setbacks. Knowing them will help you brace for their impact or even lessen the impacts totally. A good business plan will also help convince prospective investors to take a gamble on your ideas.

You can write your business plans yourself (highly recommended) or give them out to a professional business plan writer.

NADINE BRYANT

I have found that writing them yourself makes it easier for you to maximise all the benefits of having a business plan.

CHAPTER 3
Branding

From Microsoft to Apple, and from Gucci to Versace, every successful business is built on a brand. To the consumer, a brand is a unique identifier of value and quality. To the business, a brand is an embodiment of its goodwill. It is therefore not surprising that behind every successful brand out there, there is a story – a tale of toils over the years to improve or maintain the standards of the products or services with which a brand is associated.

While every successful brand is like Rome, which was not built in a day, the journey to that success certainly starts with a step. In this chapter of the book, I will be teaching you branding and helping you take your first step towards successfully branding your business.

What is a Brand?
A brand is a mark, symbol, logo, sign, sentence, or sound that uniquely identifies the products or services of one business from those of its competitors or other businesses. Right now, I am sure popular brand names are popping up in your head. A very good example of a brand is Coca-Cola – it is the most popular brand in the whole world. Like every other brand, Coca-Cola identifies only the products that come from the company which owns the brand.

When you combine the different types of things that can be used as a brand for your business, what you have is brand identity. As an entrepreneur, it is not an optional business practice to create a brand identity for your products or services – you **need** the branding to improve your business performance and protect your business.

Logo and Brands
Every successful business has a logo – this is a design or a sign by which the business can be recognised. A logo is a business emblem. It is a good business practice to use the logo of your business in your brand identity. This helps to prevent confusion in the market. It is, therefore important that you choose the right logo. The right logo performs two functions, one intrinsic and the other extrinsic.

The extrinsic function of a logo is to identify your business. Its intrinsic function is to attract business or sales. How can you ensure your logo performs both of these functions? The answer starts with what you choose as a logo.

If your logo is going to be an image that cannot be read, you need to make sure it nonetheless suggests the kind of business it is associated with. Choosing a sign or symbol that has no connection with the product or services of the business comes with some additional burden, such as being the first to offer such products or the need to spend a lot more on advertising.

If your logo is going to be textual, it should be in a language that your target market can read. This allows for easy identification of your goods or services. If it includes a slogan to suggest the quality of the product, it should be short, impressive, and memorable. The qualities of a logo, whether visual or textual, as described here is what is called the theme of the logo. You can create the logo yourself if you have knowledge of graphics design. If you do not, you can engage a design team to create one for you. I used "engage' because you need to properly inform them of what you want.

Brand Loyalty
As earlier explained, a brand is a unique identifier of value and quality. If your product offers satisfaction to your customers, the associated brand acquires the characteristic of giving trust and

confidence in your products. So, to build a successful brand, a brand that commands the attention, respect, and confidence of consumers, the first step is offering quality products and services. A great first experience with your brand can foster loyalty with specific customers, and more often than not, they will indirectly market your offerings by word-of-mouth. Consumers don't want to waste time sorting through the different brands of the same product out there. So, if they are satisfied with your brand, they will recommend it to others and go for it rather than your competitors. This is called brand loyalty.

Your Brand is an Asset
The trust and confidence your brand create for your goods and services have another advantage – it gives value to the brand itself, making it possible for you to use it to generate income. This is why a brand is also known as a business asset.
The income a brand can generate for you does not have to be from your own goods alone. It can also come from the goods of others whom you have given permission to use your brand. Such other persons are riding on the goodwill that your brand has and because there is no such thing as a free lunch, they pay for it. I will discuss this further when I explain how to protect your trademark.

Protecting Your Brand: Trademark
Have you ever wondered why everybody cannot use Microsoft or Pepsi in their business? The answer lies in what is called intellectual or industrial property. The law recognises that many businesses spend a lot on developing their brand and achieving a reputation of trust and confidence in the market. Therefore, in order to reward such industry and prevent such reputation from being damaged by unscrupulous players in the market, the concept of a trademark was developed.
A trademark gives your business the exclusive right to use your brand. You really do not have to wait till your brand becomes successful before you register it as a trademark. It can be registered

right from the beginning of your business.

A successful brand forms part of your business's intellectual capital. As explained earlier that it is an asset; it only becomes so when registered as a trademark. Thus, when registered, you can validly and confidently license others to use it. If an unlicensed person uses it, an infringement has occurred, and the law will require such persons to give over such products and/or whatever profits they made from such unauthorised usage to you.

What is Your Brand Story?

Every story begins with "once upon a time." Every brand has a story behind it. Some have fought to stay relevant in a fiercely competitive market. Others have fought legal battles to prevent being taken advantage of while others have fought severe financial wars to stay alive. Yet, others have never had to fight at all. Did you know Microsoft once helped Apple weather a financial storm?

There are many successful brands today in any of those categories. You are setting out right now into the business world, no longer as a consumer but as a producer. You have the opportunity to create a brand story that will last decades and centuries, and doing that starts with creating a brand. So, plan your brand story well. Do not wait for damage control to create a story. From the beginning, let your brand tell its own story.

Creating a Business Name

A business name is also a trading name. It is the name your business will be called or known by. There is a way to choose a business name, and there are consequences for whatever name you choose. I will explain the consequences in the next chapter. In this chapter, the focus is on the nexus between your business name and your brand. Your business name is part of your brand. Your business name does not necessarily mean the name in which your business is officially registered. It is usually a simple name by which you carry on your business. While your trademark should be based on your business name, your business name does not have to be your official name. Take Google as an example. It is a trademark belonging to Alphabet Inc., the official name of the U.S. company that owns it.

Your business name should, therefore, be short, simple, impressive, and memorable. It should be short because a long one prevents easy mouthing. It should be simple because if it is difficult to pronounce, it puts people off. It should be impressive so that it can attract new consumers. It should be memorable so that people can easily remember it. You should decide on at least three business names. The reason for that will be explained in the next chapter.

Build a Website

Permit me to draw your attention to what is now known as the dotcom bubble. Like all bubbles, it burst. When the Internet became open for public use, a lot of businesses discovered its potential for their business.

There was a frenzy, a scramble for space online. Investors were willing to throw money at any business so long as it had an online presence even if its ideas were not commercially feasible. When the bubble burst, many billions were lost. The lesson?

Always have a solid business plan. It was not having space online that ruined those businesses. It was lack of a solid business plan. The truth, therefore, still remains that if you ever want to be fully successful as a business, you need to secure a lot in cyberspace. That lot where your business resides online is its website, and you choose the nature of the website based on your business and goals. A website is a collection of related webpages. Below are simple and effective tips for setting up your business website.

<u>Choosing the Name</u>

On the Internet, websites are located using web addresses. A web address is a URL or a uniform resource locator. While it is actually a string of numbers, to make it easy, it is converted into the text, which starts with "www" we are all familiar with now. Your website name should be the same as your business name – this makes it easy for those who are familiar with your business from other sources to easily locate it online. Once you make sure it is the same as your chosen business name, it will have satisfied all the necessary conditions to lead to business success for you.

Choosing the Host

All websites are located on web servers around the world. These web servers are provided and administered by some businesses called web hosting platforms. They allow you to house your website on their server and administer it from there. Think of what they provide you as some kind of dashboard where you can control everything related to your website. The type of web hosting you go for depends on the type of website you need. If you are providing goods and services online for free or for a fee, your web hosting options must be different from the one to use for a simple business information website.

Simple Design

There is always the temptation of wanting to overdo things. That certainly backfires. Keep the design of your website simple. The theme and layout you choose will depend on your business and what you intend to use the website for. In all, there is one absolute rule – avoid cluttering. It makes your website slow and sometimes unresponsive. All of these put people off. Imagine if someone has to shut down their web browser because of your website. The next time, they will go looking for your competition.

Mobile friendly

Mobile internet traffic accounts for more than 50% of the total web traffic. What does that tell you? People are accessing the Internet more via their handheld devices than through a laptop or a desktop. This is why your website, no matter what function it performs, must be optimised for mobile viewing. Luckily, your optimisation comes preinstalled on all web hosting platforms. But a little tweaking may be required to set you above your rivals.

Call to action

This is good for lead generation. Every person who visits your website deliberately or mistakenly is a potential customer. You must not allow them to go without leaving a way for you to contact them later. This is where "call to action" comes in. Offer things such people will be interested in and ask them to drop their emails to claim the rewards or sign up for your newsletter.

Contact info
Whatever type of website you run, you must not forget to add the "Contact Us" menu. This is even more important if your business depends on direct interaction between your salespersons and consumers. And do not just leave contact information on your website. Do make sure to be responsive, too. Internet users talk – you should not be surprised that unresponsive websites gain negative traction in internet forums.

Blog and Social media
Your website should contain a blog – a section that features daily or weekly updates from you. Think of it as your business's open or public journal. Share ideas with people using your blog, and by the time you develop a wide readership, your website becomes optimised for search engines. Don't even think of neglecting social media. Apart from having a website, you need to also be on social media platforms. If people are not googling, they are on social media posting, liking, commenting, and retweeting. Your website should link visitors with your social media pages, and your social media pages should link followers back to your website.

Maintenance
Finally, make it a habit to update and upgrade your website. Both of these are not provided just for the fun of it. They are necessary to keep the machinery running.
While there are several tools out there to help you create your website on your own, nothing stops you from hiring a professional to do it for you.
Your brand is the soul of your business – it is the identity you project and the name by which you are addressed. Therefore, it is

important to have the right branding.

CHAPTER 4
Registering your business

The law is an intrusive concept – it never leaves humans alone, not even in death. The law regulates all of our affairs and online businesses are no exceptions. Apart from the organisation that business law creates in the business world, there is also the added advantage of filtering out unscrupulous businesses and conferring legitimacy on the right ones.

This chapter is about the legitimacy of your business as achieved through registration. But, first, you need to understand the available business entities that your business may conform with under the law. Put in a simpler way, these entities are just the legal formats your business may take under the law.

Sole Trading

This is also known as a sole proprietorship. It means a business owned and run by one person called the sole trader. This type of business entity is not considered different from its owner. That means that gains, losses, and liabilities of the businesses are the gains, losses, and liabilities of the owner. This means that the owner is solely liable for the liabilities of the business.

If you are trading in your own name, there is no requirement for you to register the business name and get an Australian Business Number (ABN). If you are trading in a name other than yours, then you need to register the business name and get the ABN. Also, for the purposes of taxation, the business is not treated separately from its owner.

The income of the business is regarded as that of the owner and thus taxable as personal income. While a sole trader trading in their own name is not required to have an Australian Business Number, there is an advantage to doing so as it helps the business cut back on withholding taxes. If the turnover of your business annually exceeds AUD75,000, you become liable to pay the Goods and Services Tax.

From what I have said so far about the sole trader, you will realise that it is a business format most suitable for running a very small business where the risk is very low. You do not even have to open a separate bank account for the business as you can use your personal account for it.

Partnerships

This is a form of sole trading but with more than one person, and a maximum number of 20. That is why it is called a partnership i.e., the coming together of two or more persons for the purpose of doing business. Like sole trading, the law does not regard the partnership as a separate person from the partners who own it. In other words, the gains, losses, and liabilities of the partnership are the gains, losses, and liabilities of the partners.

A partnership is formed around a Deed of Partnership. A Deed of Partnership is a document that outlines the nature of the business, the owners (partners) of the business, the contribution of each to the capital, the entitlement of each to profit, and the ratio for sharing the losses.

However, notwithstanding the existence of a ratio for sharing losses, each partner is as answerable for the liabilities of another partner just as the wanting partner himself or herself. To avoid this, the concept of limited liability partnership was developed to limit the liability of each partner for the other's misdeeds.

A partnership will have no legal duty to register a business name if the partners are carrying on the business in their names. However, there is an advantage if they do, as I have mentioned earlier under sole trading.

If the partnership is in a name other than the names of the partners, then they must register a business name and get the Australian Business Number. A partnership has a TAX File Number – this means the partnership pays taxes. At the same time, the partners still pay personal income taxes. A partnership allows the partners to pull resources together for the purpose of the business. But unlike the sole trader, decision making is slow as partners will have to be consulted.

Incorporated Companies
When a company is incorporated, it means the law will regard that company to be a separate legal entity under the law. In other words, such a company will be regarded as different from its owners (called members or shareholders). This means the company can buy, own or sell property in its own incorporated name. The company is in law regarded as an artificial person distinct from the natural persons who own it. This artificial person called the company cannot die unless it is wound up or liquidated. This artificial person also has the power to sue another person, and another person can also sue it.

The essence of an incorporated company is that its liability is different from that of its owner. Even when a company is in debt and its owner is very rich and can afford to pay off the said debt, the creditors of the company will not be able to go after the owner. An owner of a company is only liable to the extent of the amount taken up by him or her in the company.

Company's Liability
Every company has a share capital. This is an amount of money with which the company can trade. In Australia, the amount is as low as AUD1.

Supposing you incorporate your business with AUD50,000 as the share capital. This capital will be divided into shares, and each share will have a value which, when added together, will make up the AUD50,000 capital. Our AUD50,000 can be divided into 50,000 shares at AUD1 each. In Australia, a single person can incorporate a company, but let's say there are two of you. Each of you can take 25,000 shares each.

What this means is that each of you is owing the company the sum of 25,000 * AUD1. That equals AUD25,000 for each one of you or AUD50,000 for the two of you. When these shares are issued, you have the opportunity of paying them up once and for all.

Therefore, when the company makes a profit and declares dividends, you are paid a cut from the profit as a return on your investment. Where no dividends are declared, you are not paid anything as a return on your investment.

When the company runs into financial troubles and needs to pay debts, it can call on its shares – this means the company will ask those who have not paid up for the shares issued to them to pay up. When these persons do, the company can use it to settle the debts. If it is not enough, the creditors have no option than to call for the company's assets to be liquidated and sold to cover the debts.

The above is why the most common form of business entities in the developed world is an incorporated company. It gives a satisfactory measure of insulation from business risks and liability. Hence, even investors prefer only to fund limited liability companies. Upon incorporation, a company gets an Australian Company Number, a set of 9 digits that uniquely identify every company.

Types

In Australia, there are two types of incorporated companies. The first is a Proprietary Limited Company (Pty Ltd), and the second is a Public Company. The major difference between these two entities lies in how many shareholders they can have and how they can raise capital for the business. A Proprietary Limited Company cannot have more than 50 shareholders, and it also cannot raise money from the public. It cannot advertise for investors to come and buy its shares or stocks. Also, the number of persons who can form a Pty Ltd is limited under the law. A Pty Ltd requires at least one resident director.

A Public Company can have more than 50 shareholders and is allowed to raise money from the public, hence the "public" in the name. This type of company can do this through the stock market, that is, the Australian Stock Exchange. A stock is a unit of ownership in a company, and it corresponds to a share of the company's capital. When a public company is issuing stocks to members of the public for the first time, it is said that it is having its Initial Public Offering or the IPO, which is advertised. A public company requires at least three directors, one Secretary, and a Public Officer.

Both of these companies must register for the Goods and Services Tax once the annual turnover exceeds AUD75,000. An incorporated company also has a Tax File Number because it pays companies income tax – 30% of its profits with no minimum threshold. When a shareholder is paid dividends, such is taxable as personal income. The Public Officer is responsible for paying the company's taxes.

The legal protection afforded to incorporated companies comes with a burden of reporting obligations. Such companies are also quite costly to set up. While the liability of the owner of a company is limited, as I have earlier explained, if an owner gives personal guarantees for debts, he becomes as liable as a sole trader.

Trusts
A Trust is unlike the other types of business formats discussed earlier. What a trust does is to make money and distribute it to beneficiaries. A Trust is created by a Trust Deed. The trust Deed appoints a trustee – this is a person in whom all the property of the trust will be legally vested. In other words, a trustee holds the property of the trust in its own name, trades with it, or collects the profits made from such and then distributes the profits to beneficiaries named in the Trust Deed.

A Trustee can be a natural person or an artificial person. That means an incorporated company can serve as a trustee. In fact, such companies are better as trustees than individual persons. The trustee is, of course, personally liable for its own actions. If a trust carries on business in a name other than its own, it must register the business name and obtain the Australian Business

Number. A Trust also has a Tax File Number, and distribution from the trust is treated as the taxable personal income of the beneficiaries. Like all other business entities, if the annual turnover of a trust exceeds AUD75,000 for for-profits or AUD150,000 for non-profits, it must register for the Goods and Services Tax.

Checking Business Name Availability
You will recall that I described a brand as an asset that can be protected through the legal concept of the trademark. Your business name is part of your brand, and that means just as no one else can use your business name, you also cannot use others'. Each business name is unique and exclusive to the owner. To prevent violating the rights of others, the Australian Securities and Investment Commission (ASIC) has made available a public search platform that allows you to search the business name registrar online. A brief description of how to check whether a business name is available is included below:

Log on to asic.gov.au
Click on *Business Names*
Select *Search business name register*
Select *Check business name availability* from the drop
Enter the desired business name

Three results are possible:

- The system informs you that the name is indeed available.

- The system informs you that a manual decision is needed from the government

- The system informs you that the name is not available.

Which of the structures described above should your online business follow? That will be determined by several personal factors, including the availability/absence of partners, capital available, estimated revenue, and scope of your business. By all means, you can even start with sole proprietorship and then change to a more structured entity as determined by the variable factors you come in contact with.

CHAPTER 5
Let's talk Capital Investment

How much will you need? How much you need depends on your business.

Irrespective of the type of online business you are going into, one thing is certain: you will need some capital. However, the amount of capital you will need depends on the type of business – some businesses are capital intensive while some are not.

That a business requires a lot of money to set up does not mean it will bring a lot of return on investment. In fact, a business that costs less to set up may yield more returns than one that costs much to set up. Since we agree you will need money for whatever business you want to set up, it is my aim to explain the various sources from which you can get the capital to fund your business.

Personal Savings
Funding your business from your own saving is also known as bootstrapping. It is most common and undoubtedly the easiest way to fund a business. In fact, whether you are setting up your online business as an incorporated company, a partnership, or sole trading, some amount of your money will still go into the capital. However, bootstrapping is more commonly used to fund sole trading where the other things the business will need, such as skills and time, can be provided by you. You also fund your business personally when you want to maintain total control of it.

While bootstrapping may have the advantage of eliciting more commitment from you to the business, the downside is usually reflected in the usual slow growth of the business. But what else can you do when you cannot convince someone else to trust you with their money? You fund your business yourself. And, yes, there are many successful businesses funded from the savings of the founders.

Bank loans
Taking a bank loan to fund your business idea is another option. Banks are in the business of giving loans, and their gains on such loans is the interest you pay along with the principal amount. Since the bank will not be running the business with you, they need to make sure you will be able to pay back the loan, principal, and interest, whenever the time arises. They do this by making you give security for the loan.

Security is just something valuable which the bank can sell or convert to its own (foreclose) to recover the loan, principal, and interest, in case you default on paying back at the appointed time. The loan given to you is therefore usually based on the value of the security you are offering for it. The security can be any property of value, such as a house, a piece of art, copyright, or even shares in another company.

While the bank is always willing to offer loans to people indicating the availability of funds for your business, the risk of taking loans is generally high. Even when the business goes south due to no fault of yours, the bank will still come for the loan to be repaid.

Business Grants
Business grants, from public and private bodies, are another way to fund your online business idea. Every government in the world provides such grants to small-to-medium enterprises at various stages, whether at the beginning or for purposes of expansion. The major advantage of funding your business through grants is that there is, in most cases, no requirement for you to pay back and even if there is, the interest to be repaid will be smaller compared to taking a loan from a bank. A major obstacle of such grants, however, is that you will have to meet strict requirements to be entitled to them. If it is a private body giving such grants,

you may be required to compete with others to win it. To find such grants, you may want to check out the official pages of the Australian government or simply google them.

Angel investors and Venture Capitalists

Compared with a venture capitalist, an angel investor is a benign investor in your business idea. Angel investors usually come from close family and friends who are wealthy. They are described as benign because they do not come with all the strict requirements of venture capitalists. They are not usually interested in how you run the business. They try to understand your business idea, and if they are convinced, they take a leap of faith on you.

A venture capitalist, on the other hand, has very strict requirements before putting their money in your business. In fact, they are not usually in the business on a long-term basis. They only invest in limited liability companies and once the company has its IPO, they sell their stocks and exit the company. Unlike an angel investor, a venture capitalist will require all forms of due diligence. Venture capitalism is not evil – in fact, it has been used to fund many successful businesses, especially in the technology industry.

The advantage of the two is that the angel investor or the venture capitalist will usually provide you with the needed guidance and connections you may need in your industry. They both own a part of your business – the angel investor usually owns less, and a venture capitalist usually owns more. With the latter later exiting the business after the IPO, you may eventually lose control of the business to others.

Crowdfunding

Crowdfunding is not actually an entirely new concept. It is, in fact, just another instance of applying technology to old ideas. Communities have always funded projects from time immemorial, and this is where crowdfunding falls, albeit with the added advantage of the Internet, which makes the pool of persons who can pitch in larger.

Put simply, crowdfunding is when your business is funded by generous donors who are convinced you are up to some good with it. How does it work?

First, you need to sign up on a crowdfunding platform. Then you create a project and try to convince people of its viability. This is called a campaign. If donors are convinced about your project, they contribute to it within a specific time, usually sixty days. In return, they do not own the business with you. They may only be rewarded with early releases of the product when it is available.

The obvious advantage of crowdfunding is that you are getting someone who will not share ownership of your business with you to fund it. Also, your business gets some exposure during the campaign, and that will allow you to measure its viability when eventually implemented. A great downside of this method of funding is that your business idea can get easily stolen by others.

Credit cards

Yes, you read that right. You can fund your business with a credit card. They are "credit cards" because they allow you to draw money more than is contained in your account. Of course, you will have to pay back, albeit with interest. Now, how is that different from taking a bank loan? Well, there is a limit to your credit card expenditures. Since business involves taking risks and returns cannot be guaranteed, funding it with credit cards may not be the most ideal as you may end up racking up more credit card debts than you anticipate.

Small side hustle – eBay, Gumtree, Craig's List

Lastly, a little side hustle may help you raise money for funding your business. This point still goes back to bootstrapping. While you may not have the required amount to fund your business in savings, you may nonetheless be able to raise it by selling off some of your old stuff or stuff which you are sure you do not need. All you need do is some decluttering, and you will be surprised by how many stuff you will come up with that you do not need. After determining which items need to go, you can sell them off on platforms like eBay, Craig's List, and Gumtree.

CHAPTER 6
Accounting and Banking

I have earlier explained in this book that whatever business format you adopt has consequences such as the need to get an ABN or an ACN or appoint a Tax Officer. While an ABN may not be required for sole traders, partnerships, and trusts trading in their names, it is in other cases. Every company incorporated in Australia, remember, will be given an Australian Company Number upon successful incorporation. You should, however, know that it is more beneficial to register your business with ASIC. Only a sole trader is not required to have a business account. Other business formats need to.

Being registered with ASIC means whoever will be interacting with your business will do so with a sense of security that they are not dealing with unscrupulous businesses. Such persons will also take you more seriously if you transact your business through a business account. In this chapter, I will be teaching you about the process of setting up a business account and dealing with other financial obligations.

Setting up a business bank account
Step One:
You need to register your business with ASIC. This is because you need the ABN or the ACN to open a business account.

Step Two:
You need to determine the type of business account you need. There are three types, and they are meant for different purposes.
The first is a business checking account, which is used for the daily transactions of the business, such as cash deposits by customers and withdrawals by the owner.
The second is a business savings accounts which can be used to save your profits from the business and obtain interests from the bank.
The third is a business term deposit account, which is used to fix money for a period at a fixed interest rate. You can only withdraw money from this account before the expiration of the term by paying a penalty.
Step Three
Finally, you need to decide which bank you want your business account to be domiciled with. The Australia Big Four – the four largest banks in Australia – have wide country coverage, so you may want to consider them. While these banks allow you to start the registration process online, you can only complete it in person in one of their branches.
The reason for that is that the law requires the identity of the owner of every bank account to be fully verified to prevent and detect criminal activities like money laundering and crime and terror financing. Therefore, each bank will require specific government-issued identification documents from you. When you have made a bank choice, go to their website and confirm the requirements for opening the type of account you want.

Investing in a basic accounting package
Having a business account different from your personal one helps you separate business transactions from personal ones. That al-

lows you to measure the performance of your online business, to see whether you are closer to your goals or not. Monitoring the incomes and expenditures of your business in the modern world has been made easier by technology designed explicitly for that purpose.

There are several basic accounting applications, mobile, and desktop to help you keep an organised business account. Whichever one you want to settle on must satisfy some conditions.

First, does it do what you want? You can only know this by reading the reviews of the application from various reliable sources. I will recommend professional sources as those from anonymous ones may be very doubtful.

Two, is it easy to use? Not all those applications are designed for all persons. Some are designed with professionals in mind.

Three, does it offer backup? This is important because you do not want to risk losing your business data.

Four, does it support transactions in multiple currencies? Since you are going to be taking your business or services online, you should know you can have foreign customers.

Five, is it compatible with other similar apps? There are instances where you may want to export business data from one app to another. If the two are not compatible, you will be stuck.

Six, is it available on all platforms? You may want to reconsider if the app you are choosing is only available on Windows and iOS. You may want to change Operating systems and so, if the app is not on all platforms, moving may become difficult or impossible.

Seven, consider the price. That it is free, cheap or expensive does not mean it is the best out there.

Take your time and choose wisely.

Tax accountant

Taxes are inevitable. You cannot legally escape them, but you legally reduce just how much of it you can pay. I have explained some of the tax implications of running a business earlier. If you do not understand the nitty-gritty of taxes, it is about time you invested in consulting a tax accountant regularly.

A good business should keep meticulous accounts and conform to all accounting and tax laws. That applies to even online businesses.

CHAPTER 7
Marketing

I have already described a bit of this under branding, but it is so important that it requires a chapter of its own.

How do you recognise a KFC outlet anywhere in the world? The iconic man in a white suit in the KFC logo does a good job, doesn't it? Well, you would walk past KFC if it had no logo or sign proclaiming its name. Taking off the name would also see a downturn in revenue for that particular outlet. Why? Fewer people would associate the KFC standards with it.

The same thing will happen to your business if you do not promote and market it. There are millions of businesses on the Internet, and yours is just another brand in your niche. To stay afloat and competitive, you need to be out there in front, creating visibility. If you sell books online, you want your titles to be the first to pop up on search engine results. You want to rank highly and make organic sales. Almost always, more visibility equals more profits and more revenue for you. That is why big brands dedicate a small fortune to promotion and sponsorship of widely-viewed events to gain even more traction.

Now, you may not be prepared to battle the biggest brands for advert space during the Rugby World Cup, but the Internet has given you a chance. By understanding the rules of social engine optimisation, search engine marketing, and social engagement, you can create great followership online.

What are the options available for promoting and marketing your business?

Social media

Social media is the largest community on Planet Earth. Every individual on social media is just one button or hashtag away from knowing about you and your brand. You can try to drive organic engagements through great content and direct copywriting.

For instance, if you want to gain credence as a life coach, you may choose to answer questions about your niche on Quora, or craft genuinely engaging content about topical issues. People get to see this and become interested in your brand. You have brought the brand to them.

At the bare minimum, get active on Twitter, Facebook, and Instagram – they are the largest communities for interaction, and you can maximise them without paying a cent.

Hashtags are also important, especially on Twitter and Instagram. Hashtags can help you leverage on the pulling power of other accounts you have an agreement with. They serve as a form of keyword that can describe your brand.

YouTube is also a great platform for promoting your brand through videos; Snapchat is another.

The biggest brands are all on social media, engaging their followers and receiving feedback. Why shouldn't you be?

<u>Paid Social Media Ads</u>

If organic sales do not bring in a direct increase in engagement, it is time to switch to paid Ads. Paid Ads perform better because you are paying the social media platform to advertise your brand. The more people see and interact with your brand, the more the platform can charge you. So, they are partners in a way.

With such vested interests, paid Ads often convert better than organic Ads. Most social media platforms will charge you on a Pay

Per Click basis – meaning you pay only when people click the Ads. All you need to do is select your budget and monitor your Ads, and the platform will try to find the best matches for your Ads.

Email and Direct messaging
Good old email copy still sells any day. It may no longer be the rave it once was, but a dedicated email list can give you a boost, especially if the leads you send emails to, are interested in your niche. To execute this, you may need some great copywriting skills or hire a copywriter to help you select the appropriate words to sell your brand.

Blogging
Every serious online business should have a website with a blog for engaging their leads. Why? Your blog will naturally attract people if the content is catchy and educative. It will also attract leads that are genuinely interested in what you do. Things get even better when you consider the fact that you can even earn from blogging in addition to what your business does. Google's AdSense and affiliate commissions are two major ways for monetising your blog and turning it into an extra source of revenue for your business.

The Three Pillars of Your Marketing Campaign
Regardless of the kind of marketing campaign you have chosen, you need to pay attention to three things that will determine how well your campaign is received and the returns in the visible impact that it generates.

- **Content**

Content refers to what goes into your Ads and campaigns. It could be written, audio, or video content – whatever it is, your aim is to pique the curiosity of your followers and keep them stuck to you for long enough to pass your brand message. Content can take any form. It may be educative, sponsored or even controversial. So, focus on creating enthralling content that can keep readers hooked. Content is king any day.

- **Engagement**

Engage your customers. Provide access for them to reach you. That may be via comments, reviews, or even email feedback. The aim is to ensure that you put a human face to the whole business. Let them feel like your business is alive, and adapting to meet their needs, fears, worries, and complaints. Be out there interacting with them, and you will create more loyal followers. Learn to use hashtags and keywords to promote your business and generate more engagements.

Apply SEO

You need to apply the best search engine optimisation principles, though, to keep your blog visible. What does that mean?

Most people who want a particular thing often end up looking them up on search engines such as Google and Bing. These search engines index millions of websites and try to match the best fits for every search.

If someone types "Coffee shop" into their Google search bar, for instance, Google will scour its indexed websites to look for the best fits and display them in order of priority. That's where SEO comes on. Websites and blogs with the best content (as determined by SEO) are shown first, and since the average user simply browses through the first few choices, it is important to rank highly on search results. To do this, you can learn SEO principles and the use of keywords, or you can hire a professional SEO expert for that. SEO can make or mar a website and should be paid attention to.

Marketing calls attention to what you have to offer. It tells the world where you are and what your services are. It helps you reach the whole world at the touch of a button. It is key to building a loyal customer base that stays loyal to your brand.

CHAPTER 8
Staying the Course

Now that you have the required knowledge to start your business, how can you sustain and maintain the initial momentum? For many business owners, this is the deal-breaker. They start with great ideas and good plans, but they still fizzle out after a few weeks. What can you do to avoid this fate?

There are three things to do actually.

i. Focus on Growing your Empire

ii. Delve deeply into self-development

iii. Review/Reassess Goals at each milestone

- Focus on Growing your Empire

In business, you are either growing or losing ground. Every minute spent in stagnation is a minute lost to your competitors. There is no mercy – everyone is out for a fatter slice of the market share. If you stay still for too long, you will get knocked over and out of the game. Of course, mindless and purposeless expansion doesn't work either, but staying in your comfort zone has great psychological effects on you. You must always be on the lookout for new ways to move closer to your clients and new methods to improve your service delivery. There is always room for improvement, and you must always search for this room. When you think you have gotten to the peak of a goal, you can always expand outwards for more goals to improve your brand.

Do you want an empire? Well, you have to continue building the castles and kingdoms that will make up the empire.

- Delve deeply into self-development – courses, seminars, mastermind,

Women are great learners. We pick things fast and hold onto them. So, the only way you are not picking new things and improving is if you aren't looking in the right places. Self-development has to be at the forefront of your search – just as your brand has room for growth, on a personal note, you also have room to grow. Self-improvement is a lifelong commitment to constant, marginal increase in capacity and personal ability – and it is one thing you cannot afford to shirk.

Luckily, there are tons of webinars and courses out there that can help you with self-improvement. You can even amass more technical skills from these webinars and courses. In the same way you are dedicated to your business, you should create time to improve technically and personally.

- Review/Reassess Goals at each milestone

The story of *Blackberry and Nokia* is a curious one. Just about a decade ago, *Blackberry* and *Nokia* held substantial shares of the smartphone market. Today, one is no longer a thing, and the other barely exists as a shadow of itself. What happened?

Both giants lost sight of their broader goal, which one would assume to be to serve the interest of their customers. They became engrossed in pushing trends that the market had clearly rejected. The results were disastrous and plain to see. *Nokia* has been able to dam some of the impacts and remains afloat, however *Blackberry* has disappeared into oblivion. That's what happens when you lose sight of your overall destination – you get punished in the cruellest way possible.

No market or business industry is ever going to stay still. You need to constantly audit your goals and plans to ensure you are not going against the market. Nobody goes against the market for long enough without suffering its consequences. Therefore, you must be ready to review your goals at every milestone.

Do they still conform to your broad vision?

Do they go against what market trends are saying?

What has changed that makes your plan inaccurate?

Continue to readjust and reassess your plans and smaller goals, or they will never sum up to the main goal you have. In the online business world, change is the only constant. Sway and bend with new advancements, techniques, and market forces, or the gale may break you.

CONCLUSION

So, there you have it. Your step-by-step guide to building your online business. Piece of cake, right?! Ha. Kidding! We all know it takes hard work and persistence, but I hope this book has given you the confidence to take the first step to building your empire. The next step is to follow the guide and start implementing the steps to turn your passion into your empire. Revisit the book as many times as you need to refresh your memory and keep you focused.

If you enjoyed the book, I would greatly appreciate if you would leave a review on Amazon.

Thanks again for taking the time to read this book, it truly means a lot to me. If you feel this book will benefit anyone you know, please feel free to pass *Business As Usual* to any aspiring female entrepreneurs.

If you'd like to hear more from me, please check me out at **www.frompassiontoempire.com** and subscribe to my blog for weekly updates.

With love,
Nadine